To Shelly, Leo, Christina, and especially to YOU, the reader; may this book fuel your curiosity and wonder. —C.P.

Published by National Geographic Partners, LLC, Washington, DC 20036.

Copyright © 2025 National Geographic Partners, LLC.

All rights reserved. Reproduction of the whole or any part of the contents without written permission from the publisher is prohibited.

NATIONAL GEOGRAPHIC and Yellow Border Design are trademarks of the National Geographic Society, used under license.

MARVEL, the MARVEL logo, IRON MAN and related properties are trademarks and/or copyrights, in the United States and other countries, of MARVEL and/or its affiliates. © 2025 MARVEL.

Designed by Gustavo Tello

Trade paperback ISBN: 978-1-4263-7515-6
Reinforced library binding ISBN: 978-1-4263-7556-9

The author and publisher gratefully acknowledge the literacy review of this book by Mariam Jean Dreher, professor emerita of reading education, University of Maryland, College Park, and expert review by Tim Murphy and Carlos Villa of the National High Magnetic Field Laboratory.

Art Credits
Illustrated by Ron Lim with colors by Israel Silva

Photo Credits
AS= Adobe Stock; SS=Shutterstock

ALL MARVEL CHARACTERS, ARTWORK, AND LOGOS © 2025 MARVEL

Cover: (magnet), d1sk/AS; (screw bolt), Adeus Buhai/AS; (paper clip), Ilya Podoprigorov/AS; (nails), Achira22/AS; (nail), Antti Karppinen/AS; (lightning), d1sk/AS; 1 (lightning), d1sk/AS; 1 (BACKGROUND), ArtBackground/AS; 1 (magnet), d1sk/AS; 1 (UP LE), Mark Garlick/Science Source; 1 (UP RT), pressmaster/AS; 1 (LO), New Africa/AS; 6-7, Uros Petrovic/AS; 8-9, Siberian Art/SS; 10, Gustavo Tello/National Geographic Partners, LLC; 11 (UP), Gustavo Tello/National Geographic Partners, LLC; 13 (UP), kolesnikovserg/AS; 13 (CTR), Tetra Images/Getty Images; 13 (LO), Anatoly Repin/AS; 17, Science Source; 18-19, vchalup/AS; 20 (UP), BillionPhotos/AS; 20 (CTR), Delmas Lehman/AS; 20 (LO RT), Marcello Bertinetti/Science Source; 21 (UP), michelangeloop/SS; 21 (CTR), Michael LaMonica/SS; 21 (LO), NASA/JPL-Caltech/SwRI/MSSSNASA/Kevin M. Gill; 26 (LO), pressmaster/AS; 27 (LE), Montri Thipsorn/AS; 27 (RT), Mark Garlick/Science Source; 28 (RT), Colin Wheeler/National Geographic Partners, LLC; 29 (UP LE), Colin Wheeler/National Geographic Partners, LLC; 29 (UP RT), Colin Wheeler/National Geographic Partners, LLC; 29 (LO), Colin Wheeler/National Geographic Partners, LLC; 30 (UP), showcake/AS; 30-31, max dallocco/AS; 31 (LO), michelangeloop/SS; 32 (compass), 9dreamstudio/AS; 32 (magnet), New Africa/AS; 32 (metal), Aleksandr Matveev/AS; 32 (force), Mikkel Juul Jensen/Science Source; 32 (magnetic field), Andrea Danti/AS; 32 (poles), alexlmx/AS

Printed in the United States of America
24/WOR/1

Contents

At Avengers Tower	4
What Is a Magnet?	6
Poles	8
Amazing Attraction	10
Invisible Force Field	16
6 Super Facts About Magnets	20
Back at the Lab	22
Follow the Magnet	26
Stark Industries at Home: Compass	28
Quiz Whiz	30
Glossary	32

AT AVENGERS TOWER

TONY STARK TRIES ON A NEW IRON MAN SUIT. IT IS MADE OUT OF IRON—HE IS IRON MAN, AFTER ALL!

THERE'S TROUBLE IN NEW YORK CITY! AVENGERS ASSEMBLE!

THOR RUSHES INTO THE SCIENCE LABORATORY.

THOR TRIPS OVER A CORD AND CRASHES INTO TONY'S DESK. A HORSESHOE-SHAPED OBJECT FLIES THROUGH THE AIR AND LANDS ON TONY'S NEW SUIT.

CLANG

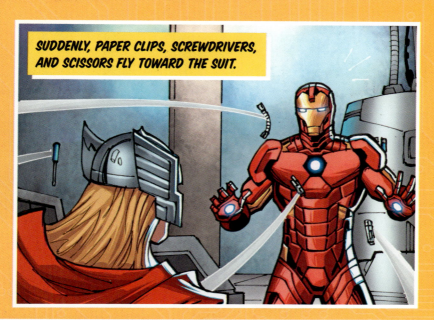

What Is a Magnet?

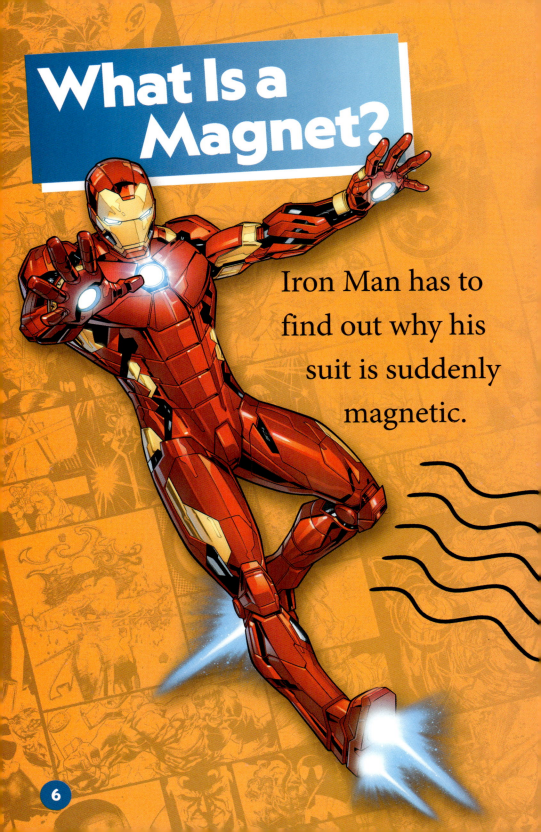

Iron Man has to find out why his suit is suddenly magnetic.

A magnet is made from a special kind of metal or rock. Magnets can pull some metals together. This is called attraction. Magnets can also push some metals apart. This is called repulsion. A magnet's power to push and pull is called magnetic force.

MAGNET: A rock or metal that can pull special metals toward it or push them away

METAL: A shiny material found in rocks that electricity and heat can go through

FORCE: A push or pull on an object

Poles

Planet Earth is one big magnet. Its center is made of iron. Earth has north and south magnetic poles. These poles are the opposite of the North and South Poles! A magnet's force is strongest at its poles.

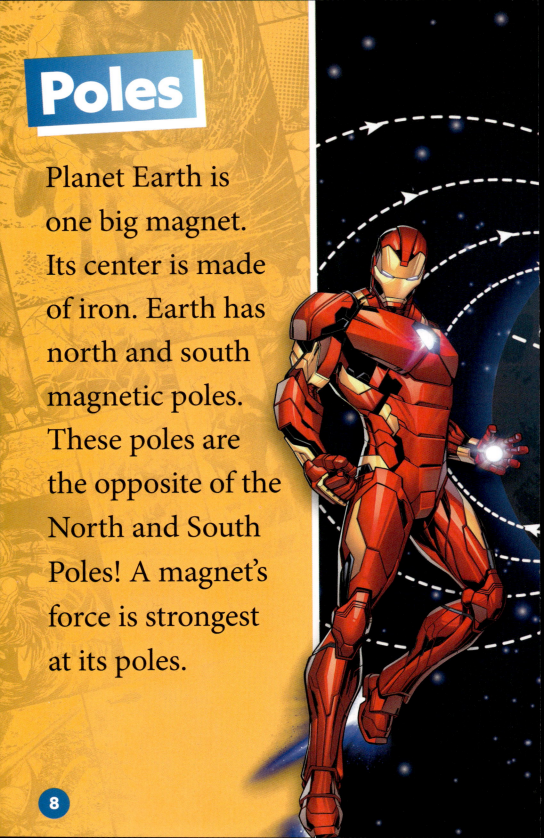

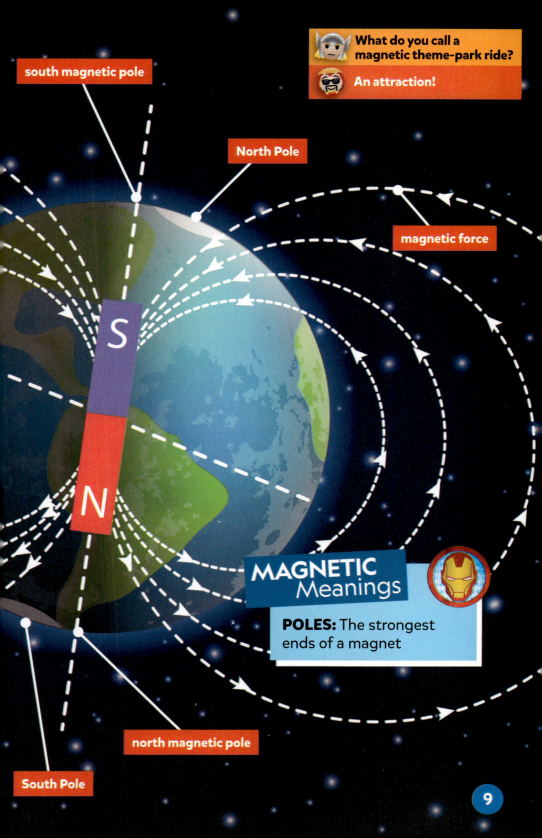

Amazing Attraction

What happens if a magnet's north pole and another magnet's south pole are next to each other? They attract and come together—just like the paper clips and Iron Man's suit.

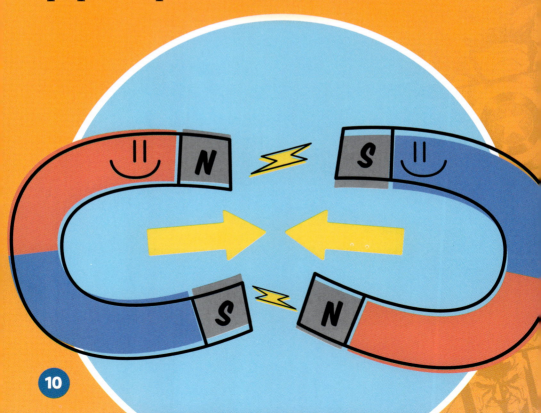

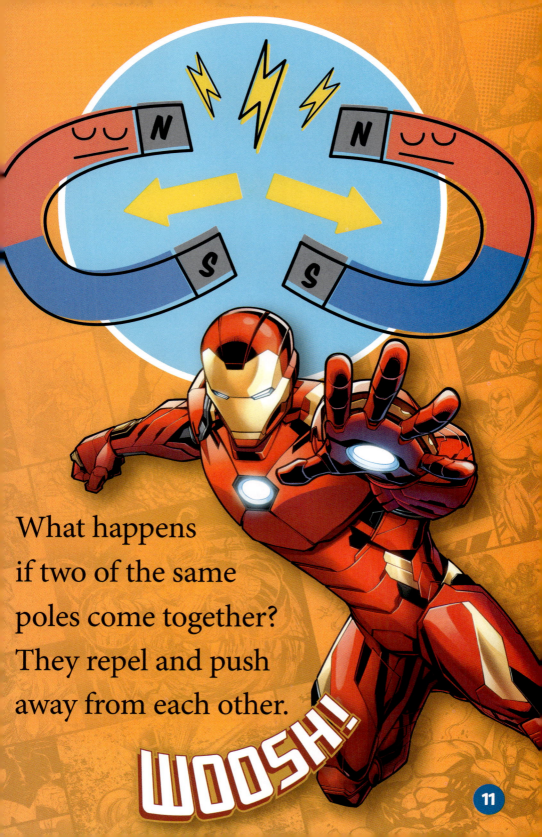

What happens if two of the same poles come together? They repel and push away from each other.

WOOSH!

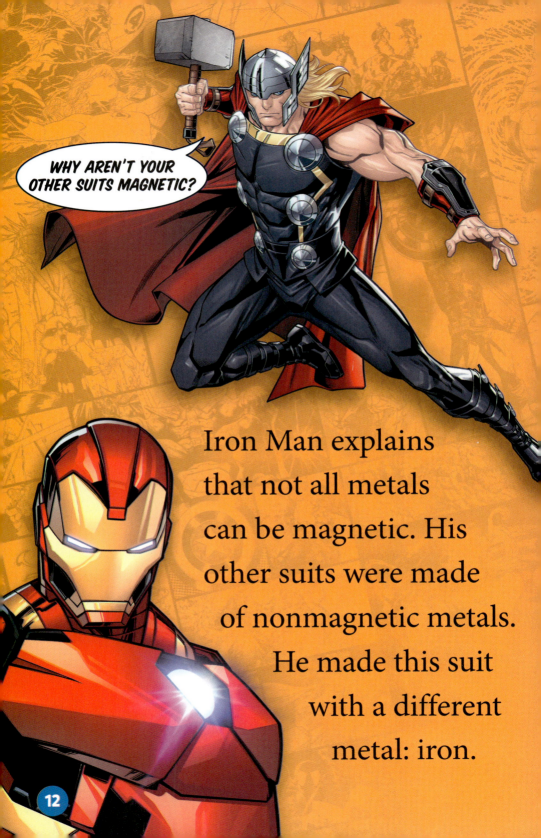

Iron Man explains that not all metals can be magnetic. His other suits were made of nonmagnetic metals. He made this suit with a different metal: iron.

Iron, nickel, and cobalt are three metals that can be magnetic. Scientists call these metals ferromagnetic. This means that they have the super-power to become magnets.

Iron is used in some pots and pans.

Nickel is used in some coins.

Cobalt is used to make batteries.

Aha! Iron Man's new suit is ferromagnetic. When Thor knocked the horseshoe-shaped magnet into the suit, it magnetized the suit. Iron Man has a new super-power: magnetism!

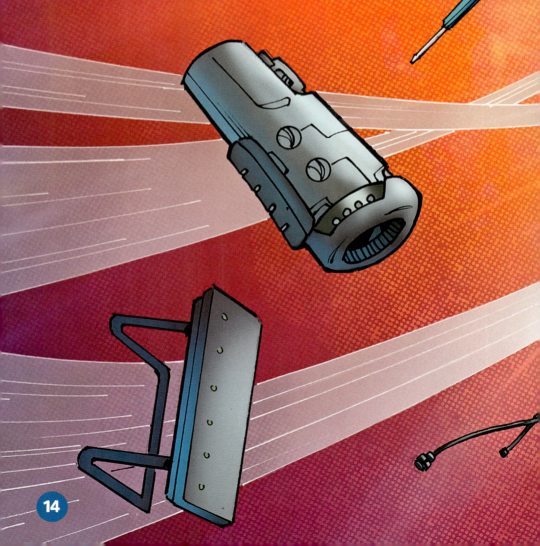

What do you call Iron Man between two magnets?
Tony Stuck!

But how powerful is his magnetic suit?

Invisible Force Field

It's time to experiment! Iron Man puts tiny pieces of iron called iron filings all over a big table. He places his magnetic metal glove over them. The filings begin to move!

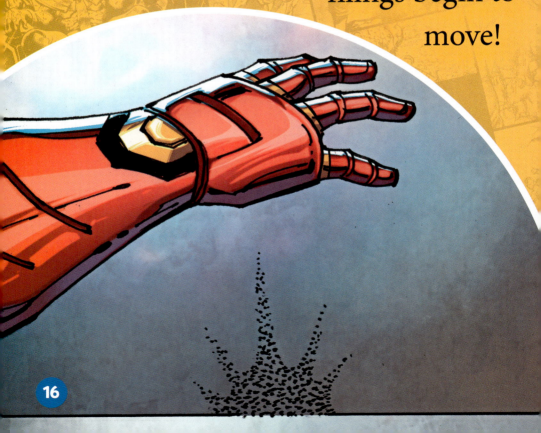

When a magnet is nearby, some filings travel from the north pole to the south pole. Others move quickly away from the poles. Whoa! The moving filings show a huge magnetic field!

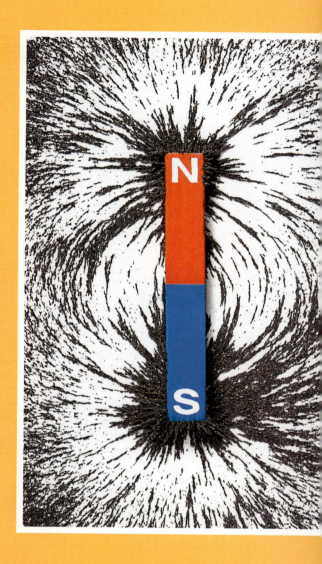

MAGNETIC FIELD: The area around a magnet that has a magnetic force

Every magnet has an invisible magnetic field around it—even Earth! Magnetic fields can be big or small, strong or weak.

Really strong magnetic fields can even work in water, through a wooden table, or in outer space!

What is a magnet's favorite Olympic sport? Pole-vaulting!

Iron Man's suit has a strong magnetic field.

6 SUPER Facts About Magnets

1 SOME BREAKFAST CEREALS CONTAIN ENOUGH IRON THAT PIECES OF THE CEREAL ARE ATTRACTED TO A STRONG MAGNET.

2 BIRDS AND SHARKS USE EARTH'S MAGNETIC FIELD TO FIND THEIR WAY.

3 SOME HIGH-SPEED TRAINS USE MAGNETIC FORCE TO "FLOAT" ABOVE THE TRAIN TRACKS.

4 A THEREMIN IS AN INSTRUMENT THAT HAS ITS OWN MAGNETIC FIELD AND CAN BE PLAYED WITHOUT BEING TOUCHED!

5 THE OLDEST MAGNETIC STONE IS THE LODESTONE.

6 JUPITER HAS THE LARGEST MAGNETIC FIELD OF ALL THE PLANETS IN THE SOLAR SYSTEM.

Where do magnets run?

 On a magnetic field.

THIS MAGNETIC SUIT IS KEEPING THE AVENGERS FROM SAVING NEW YORK CITY!

LUCKILY, IRON MAN KNOWS JUST HOW TO MAKE A MAGNET LOSE ITS MAGNETIC FIELD—BY HITTING IT!

THOR TAKES HIS HAMMER AND GIVES THE SUIT A BIG THWACK!

KRAKOOM

Follow the Magnet

Compasses have helped people find their way around the world for thousands of years.

How does a compass work? The pointer in a compass is made of magnetized metal. The pointer spins to line up with Earth's magnetic field. This means that the pointer will always point toward Earth's North Pole.

COMPASS: A tool that finds direction by using a magnetic needle to point north

Stark Industries at Home: Compass

Experiment with magnetism like Tony Stark and make your own compass!

Materials: bowl, water, paper clip, magnet, plastic bottle cap

1

Fill the bowl with water.

What do you use to catch a magnetic force?

A mag-NET!

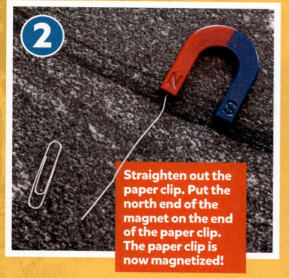

2 Straighten out the paper clip. Put the north end of the magnet on the end of the paper clip. The paper clip is now magnetized!

3 Float the bottle cap on the water in the bowl. Balance the magnetized paper clip on top of the bottle cap.

4 Watch as the magnetized paper clip end turns and stops. It's pointing in the direction of Earth's North Pole. You've made a compass!

FIND AN ADVENTURE AND BE A HERO!

QUIZ WHIZ

How much do you know about magnets? After reading this book, probably a lot! Take this quiz and find out.

Answers are at the bottom of page 31.

1 When two opposite sides of a magnet are close, they _____ each other.
A. repel
B. do not affect
C. attract
D. spin

2 The three magnetic metals are:
A. calcium, magnesium, phosphate
B. iron, nickel, cobalt
C. gold, silver, bronze
D. solid, liquid, gas

3 Earth is a giant:
A. ball of glass
B. asteroid
C. marble
D. magnet

4

Magnetic fields can work:
- A. in water
- B. in space
- C. through a wooden table
- D. all of the above

5

To the human eye, the forces in a magnetic field are:
- A. invisible
- B. pink
- C. fluffy
- D. visible

6

Which instrument can be played without being touched?
- A. piano
- B. guitar
- C. theremin
- D. xylophone

7

People have used this to find their way for thousands of years.
- A. a compass
- B. clouds
- C. a phone
- D. GPS

Answers: 1. C; 2. B; 3. D; 4. D; 5. A; 6. C; 7. A

GLOSSARY

COMPASS: A TOOL THAT FINDS DIRECTION BY USING A MAGNETIC NEEDLE TO POINT NORTH

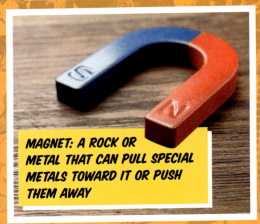

MAGNET: A ROCK OR METAL THAT CAN PULL SPECIAL METALS TOWARD IT OR PUSH THEM AWAY

METAL: A SHINY MATERIAL FOUND IN ROCKS THAT ELECTRICITY AND HEAT CAN GO THROUGH

FORCE: A PUSH OR PULL ON AN OBJECT

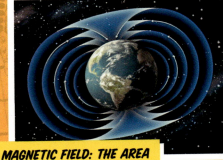

MAGNETIC FIELD: THE AREA AROUND A MAGNET THAT HAS A MAGNETIC FORCE

POLES: THE STRONGEST ENDS OF A MAGNET

32